Thomas S Cree

A Criticism of the Theory of Trades' Unions

Thomas S Cree

A Criticism of the Theory of Trades' Unions

ISBN/EAN: 9783744734158

Printed in Europe, USA, Canada, Australia, Japan

Cover: Foto ©ninafisch / pixelio.de

More available books at **www.hansebooks.com**

OF THE

THEORY OF TRADES' UNIONS.

BY

C. . . E E

GLASGOW:
PRINTED BY BELL & BAIN, 41 MITCHELL STREET.
1891.

A CRITICISM

OF THE

THEORY OF TRADES' UNIONS:

𝔄 𝔭𝔞𝔭𝔢𝔯

READ BEFORE THE ECONOMIC SCIENCE SECTION OF THE
PHILOSOPHICAL SOCIETY OF GLASGOW,
12TH NOVEMBER, 1890,

BY T. S. CREE.

———◦•◦———

UNTIL about twenty years ago most economical authorities were agreed in condemning trades' unions as a means of improving the position of the working classes. Since that time a change has taken place in the opinion of the economists, and following upon that, in the feeling of the general public towards those organisations. The laws against combination have been abolished, and many, if not most, people are now inclined to admit that trades' unions have done something for their members and their class, and that, when conducted with moderation and fairness, they are not hurtful to the commonwealth. Recent events, however, and more particularly the developments of what is called the new unionism, are now causing many to doubt the soundness of this new view, and the time seems opportune for stating the criticisms and objections of those who, like myself, have taken an interest in the question during all these years, and have never been able to accept the arguments upon which the change of opinion is based.

When, therefore, our Secretary asked me to put on paper the views which I had expressed last year in the discussion which followed Mr. Llewellyn Smith's lecture on the great Dock Strike, I readily agreed to do so.

1

Political economy is now a much more complicated study than it was in the days of Adam Smith or even of John Stuart Mill. For instance, Professor Marshall's new book on the principles of economics is full of refinements, of limitations and exceptions, of subsidiary laws which were not thought of by the earlier writers; and in the explanation of these bye-ways there seems to me to be some danger of the main road being occasionally lost sight of. As the study becomes more difficult, there is a greater probability of students accepting the arguments of their teachers as authoritative, without taking the trouble to verify them and think for themselves. There is, therefore, likely to be some advantage in outsiders occasionally reviewing dogma and argument in the light of experience, and experience is particularly valuable where principles are sought to be applied, and a certain course of action tested by them. As one who has had a good deal of experience of the working of trades' unions, and has given the subject some attention, I may be able to point out to some of you who are more accomplished economists than I am, some practical element which has been overlooked.

If, in the following remarks, I have to criticise unfavourably some of the means taken by the working-classes to attain their ends, I need hardly say that I do not do so in any spirit of antagonism to the workmen. I have as much sympathy with working people and their desire to better themselves as any man can have, and it is for that reason that I feel called upon to speak out when I see them taking what I think to be wrong methods, more likely to hurt than to better their condition.

I do not intend to speak of trades' unions as benefit societies; there is no fault to find with them there, though it may be doubted whether there is any advantage in special or provident societies being attached to each trade. Nor do I deny—what is perhaps rather much insisted upon—that trades' unions have some educative advantages. These advantages are common to all organisations, whether sound in principle or the reverse, and in this case are more than counterbalanced by the loss of independent thought and action.

I confine my criticism of trades' unions to the question whether their action is a legitimate and efficient means of raising wages. I will try to avoid the use of any expression which can give offence to any trades-unionist, as far as that is consistent with a plain statement of my opinions.

Mr. Llewellyn Smith began his lecture last year with a short exposition of the theory on which trades' union action in general is based. It is that theory which I now propose to discuss. I have not been able to get a copy of Mr. Llewellyn Smith's paper; but that is of little consequence, as the argument is the same as was first stated by Mr. John Stuart Mill in the year 1869 in two articles which he wrote for the *Fortnightly Review* in the May and June numbers of that year, reviewing Mr. Thornton's book on " Labour and its Claims." These articles are now republished in his works (" Dissertations," No. IV.)

Mr. Mill is an acknowledged authority, and a master of the art of clear exposition. His statement of the case is much fuller than Mr. Llewellyn Smith's could be ; and as his argument was adopted by Mr. Smith, and his again approved, as he told us, by Professor Marshall, I will take the former as my text, and will summarise it as fairly as I can.

In the main Mr. Mill accepts Mr. Thornton's conclusions, though he restates them in his own way.

In speaking of Mr. John Stuart Mill as a great authority, it is necessary to remember that there were two very distinct periods in his life and modes of thought. During the first period, under the influence of his father, he was a clear and cool expositor of natural laws. During the second period, under influences with which those who have read his life will be familiar, he became much more inclined to take a sentimental view of things, and some may think was too ready to accept theories which seemed to offer a way of escape from the stern operation of these laws. It is, therefore, not so bold a step, as it might appear to be, to question the conclusions of his later writings.

Up till 1869 Mr. Mill had been an opponent of any attempt to raise wages by combination. In his "Principles" he says—"The condition of the working-classes can be bettered in no other way than by altering the proportion which capital bears to population to their advantage, and every scheme for their benefit which does not proceed on this as its foundation is, for all permanent purposes, a delusion." But now he recants his former opinions.

Before proceeding to state his main argument, I may here say that I intend to confine my remarks to the question, whether trades' unions can obtain an advance of wages *out of profits*. The popular belief that there is a second source from which it is possible for an augmentation to come—namely, prices—is not held, so far as I am aware, by any economical authority, and it is, therefore, not necessary for me to discuss it.

In case, however, there are any of my hearers who hold that view, I will quote a passage from Mr. Mill's essay, to which I have referred. He says—"There cannot be a general rise of prices unless there is more money expended. But the rise of wages does not cause more money to be expended. It takes from the incomes of the masters and adds to those of the workmen; the former have less to spend, the latter have more; but the general sum of money incomes of the community remains what it was, and it is upon that sum that money prices depend. There cannot be more money expended upon everything when there is not more money to be expended altogether. A rise in general wages cannot, therefore, be compensated to the employers generally by a general rise in prices." "From the necessity of the case, the only fund out of which an increase of wages can possibly be obtained by the labouring classes, considered as a whole, is profits."

Mr. Mill elaborates this point, but that should be sufficient here.

Mr. Mill's main argument is as follows :—

Mr. Thornton has shown, by an elaborate argument and by several examples, that the law of supply and demand does not fix price with perfect exactness, or rather that supply and demand become equal, not at an exact point in price, but that it may be that several prices, or a range of prices, will satisfy the requirements of

that law; that there is or may be a kind of table land within which
the law does not operate. The typical example by which he proves
this is a sale of a hundredweight of fish by Dutch auction—that is,
the seller bidding down instead of the buyers bidding up. He
supposes that there may be only one buyer present willing to give
20s. for the lot, and no other buyer willing to give more than 18s.;
by the Dutch auction the buyer will take the offer at 20s., while by
the English auction the bidding will stop at 18s., and the man who
is willing to give 20s. will get the fish at that price, 18s., or a fraction over it. Thus, he says, " In the same market, with the same
quantity of fish for sale, and with customers in number and every
other respect the same, the same lot of fish might fetch two very
different prices," and Mr. Mill goes on to say " the law is equally
and completely fulfilled by either of these prices." Mr. Llewellyn
Smith's argument was exactly the same, his example being, according to my recollection, as follows :—

A house builder has a house for sale, for which he would like to
get £1000, but would be willing to take £950 rather than miss a
sale. And there is a buyer who would like to buy at £950, but
would, if necessary, go the length of £1000. There is thus between
£950 and £1000 a kind of no-man's-land of £50, at any point of
which the demand and supply are equal. Whether the buyer or
seller gets the larger share of that £50 depends upon astuteness in
bargaining or some accidental circumstance, and not at all on the
law of supply and demand, which is inoperative within these limits.

The principle of the two cases is exactly the same.

Mr. Mill goes on to say, " When the equation of demand and
supply leave the price indeterminate because there is more than one
price which would fulfil the law, neither buyers nor sellers are
under the action of any motives derived from supply and demand
to give way to one another. Much will in that case depend on
which side has the initiative of price. This is well exemplified in Mr.
Thornton's supposed Dutch auction. The commodity might go no
higher than 18s. if the offers came from the buyer's side, but
because they come from the seller the price reaches 20s. Now, Mr.

Thornton has well pointed out that this case, though exceptional among auctions, is normal as regards the general course of trade. As a general rule, the initiative of price does rest with the dealers. And then he goes on to say, " If it should turn out that the price of labour falls within one of the excepted cases, the case which the law of equality between demand and supply does not provide for because several prices all agree in satisfying that law, we are already able to see that the question between one of those prices and another will be determined by causes which operate strongly against the labourer and in favour of the employer. For there is this difference between the labour market and the market for tangible commodities, that in commodities it is the seller, but in labour it is the buyer, who has the initiative in fixing the price. It is the employer the purchaser of labour, who makes the offer of wages ; the dealer, who is in this case the labourer, accepts or refuses. Whatever advantage can be derived from the initiative is, therefore, on the side of the employer, and in that contest of endurance between buyer and seller, by which alone in the accepted case the price so fixed can be modified, it is almost needless to say that nothing but a close combination among the employed can give them even a chance of successfully competing against the employers."

But Mr. Mill goes on to say, " It will be said that labour is not in that barely possible excepted case. Supply and demand do entirely govern in the price obtained for labour." " This theory rests on what may be called the doctrine of the wages fund, and may be found in every treatise on political economy, my own included." And he then proceeds to state the wages fund theory, with limitations which make it no longer an operative law on one side. He concludes with these remarks, " There is no law of nature making it inherently impossible for wages to rise to the point of absorbing not only the funds which the employer intends to devote to carrying on his business, which may be called the wages fund, but the whole of what he allows for his private expenses beyond the necessaries of life. In short, there is abstractedly available for the payment of wages not only the employer's capital, but the whole of what can possibly be retrenched from his private expenditure, and the law of wages on the side of demand amounts only to the obvious proposition that the employers cannot pay away in wages what they have not got."

— "But though the population principle and its consequences are in no way touched by this, the doctrine hitherto taught by all, or most economists, including myself, which denied that trade combinations can raise wages or which limited their operation in that respect to the somewhat earlier attainment of a rise which the competition of the market would have produced without them, this doctrine is deprived of its scientific value and must be thrown aside. The power of trades' unions may, therefore, be so exercised as to obtain for the labouring classes collectively both a larger share and a larger positive amount of the produce of labour; increasing, therefore, one of the two factors on which the remuneration of the individual labourer depends. The other and still more important factor, the number of sharers, remains unaffected. On the side of supply the law, as laid down by economists, remains intact. The more numerous the competitors for employment the lower, *cæteris paribus*, will the wages be. And here comes in the necessity for considering the question raised by these restrictive rules, forbidding the employment of non-unionists, and limiting the number of apprentices which many unions maintain, and which are sometimes indispensable to the complete efficacy of unionism. For there is no keeping up wages without limiting the number of competitors for employment, and all such limitation inflicts distinct evil upon those whom it excludes, upon that great mass of labouring population which is outside the unions ; an evil not trifling, for if the system were rigorously enforced, it would prevent unskilled labourers or their children from ever rising to the condition of skilled." Mr. Mill justifies this by two considerations. First, by considering the unions of particular trades as a mere step towards a universal union including all labour, and as a means of educating the elite of the working class for such a future. And secondly, he says, " there is another and less elevated, but not fallacious point of view, from which the apparent injustice of unionism to the non-united class of labourers may be vindicated. This is the Malthusian point of view so blindly decried as hostile and odious above all to the labouring classes. The ignorant and untrained part of the poorer classes (such unionists may say) will people up to the point which will keep their wages at that miserable rate which the low scale of their ideas and habits makes endurable to them. As long as their minds remain in their present state, our preventing them from competing with us for employment does them no real injury; it only saves ourselves from being brought down to their level. Those whom we exclude are a morally inferior class of labourers to us, their labour is worth less, and their want of prudence and self restraint makes them much more active in adding to the population. We do them no wrong by intrenching ourselves behind a barrier, to exclude those whose competition would bring down our wages without more than momentarily raising theirs, but only adding to the total number in existence." I have given this passage at full length as it is an important one, and I do not wish to do Mr. Mill an injustice by compressing it.

Well, that is the theory of trades' unions as stated by Mr. Mill, and I am not aware of any fuller or more authoritative statement of the case, but to make it as complete as I can I will add one or two supplementary arguments taken from other economists.

Mr. Fawcett states that, as a matter of fact, wages do not rise immediately with an improvement in trade without the help of a trades' union, and that uncombined the men would not at first get the share of the increased profits to which they are entitled.

Professor Marshall says—"A man who employs a thousand others is in himself an absolutely rigid combination to the extent of one thousand units of buyers in the labour market." He also says—"It is certain that manual labourers, as a class, are at a disadvantage in bargaining."

And Professor Fleeming Jenkin says—"The legitimate action of a trades' union is to enable the labourer to set a reserved price on his merchandise. Each labourer who has a reserved fund may bargain for himself, and concerted action is not theoretically necessary to allow of bargaining, but practically the individual labourer seldom bargains; but acting in concert with others he can and does set a reserved price on his labour, and gets precisely the advantage that any other salesman would." And along with this I will place the statement which we see made by public men every day that, but for combination, the masters would be able to crush the men to the dust, and pay them nothing more than starvation wages.

Another plea for unionism is that it enables workmen to resist the tyranny of capital in other matters than mere wages, such as fines, arbitrary dismissal, oppressive and irritating regulations.

Professor Nicholson, in his article on wages in the *Encyclopædia Britannica*, gives his opinion that trades' unions cannot raise nominal wages much, but that their proper function is, by looking after the interests of their members in various ways, to improve their general condition, and so raise the real rate of wages.

It is also said that, as a matter of fact, trades' unions have raised wages. Finally, it is said that trades' unions can regulate the hours of labour. Our leading politicians have lately been deprecating the interference of the State with the hours of adult male labour, and have been telling the workmen that in their unions they have a far more legitimate and as effectual a means to that end.

That is the case for trades' unionism, as far as I know it.[*] I will now proceed to enquire how far it is in accordance with facts and reason.

Mr. Mill's first proposition may be admitted. Every business man knows that the law of supply and demand does not fix the terms of every particular bargain exactly. That is, indeed, a self-evident proposition, so obvious that it must have been clear to the earlier economists when discussing that law, and it is not, therefore,

---

[*] Many unionist workmen adopt and act upon the principle of doing as little work as possible so as to provide more employment for others, and some unions insist on a fixed uniform rate of output and wages, thus reducing all workers to the lowest level of efficiency, and preventing any development of skill. But in this essay I am discussing the views of educated economists, and need not do more than refer to such economical absurdities.

a new discovery which invalidates or modifies the law. There is generally such a thing as getting the worst or the best of a bargain. That is true, but it is not the whole truth. It is, indeed, a very short view of the matter. The operation of the law does not finish with the conclusion of that particular bargain. The goodness or badness of the bargain, the amount by which the price exceeds or falls below the imaginary point at which (in the old theory) demand and supply are supposed to be equal, have each their effect in stimulating or checking demand or supply for the future. In the example Mr. Mill gives of fish selling either at 18s. or 20s., the demand and supply being the same at both prices, it would still be the case that a sale at 20s. would tend to stimulate future supply and check demand, with a consequent tendency to a fall in price, while an 18s. price would tend to bring out more buyers, and reduce the inducement to go to sea. In the same way, if the house-builder got £1,000 for his house, he would be pleased with his profit and encouraged to build more houses, while buyers would be checked, and if £950 were the price, more people would think of investing in houses, while the builder would be discouraged, and not inclined to build more. The low price would, therefore, tend ultimately to a higher price, and the higher price would tend to a lower one. In other words, while Mr. Mill's argument is true as regards any particular bargain, it is untrue if a larger unit of time be taken. Over a number of cases the mean of the oscillations of price is an exact point and not a range of prices, and this is true, of course, in the wages of labour as well as in other kinds of bargains. A higher wage will bring out more labourers, and by reducing the employers' profits, will make him less anxious to employ more labour, while a lower wage has the reverse effect. The practical outcome of this argument is that, while the terms of a particular bargain are of importance to the individual workman and employer concerned, they are not of much importance to the workmen and employers as a whole, as there is always a compensating action going on which is bringing back wages to a true economical point and not to a range of prices.

There is not an inch of ground which can be called a no-man's-land within which the law of supply and demand does not operate. Every farthing of variation on the price has its effect on future supply and demand, just as every drop of water swells the sea.

The economic law works by tendency only. It approaches exactitude over a multiplicity of cases, but not in any individual case.

This consideration alone vitiates Mr. Mill's whole argument. But there are many other fallacies in the paper.

If, as Mr. Mill says, the Dutch auction is favourable to the seller, how is it that the great body of sellers, who have certainly the choice of which form they will employ, generally prefer the English auction? and where did Mr. Mill learn that, generally speaking, the initiative in naming a price is an advantage? The very reverse is the case. Mr. Mill has been misled by a single example. In the case he speaks of 20s. is got by the Dutch auction, while only 18s. would be got by the English. But the man who was willing to give 20s. might think that there were no others willing to give even 18s., and might speculate on that and wait till the bidding fell to 17s., running a risk of losing the fish altogether, for the chance of getting it at a lower figure. And in practice this is found to be so, the highest prices that buyers are willing to give being more readily reached by open competition of buyers in the English auction. The Dutch auction is chiefly but not always used in selling fish and fruit, perishable articles where speed is the desideratum, and also by fishermen who need no license. But in all or most other markets the English auction is preferred by the sellers. In some trades both forms are used.

In the wool trade, for instance, in a dull market, the seller is obliged to adopt the Dutch method, and on a brisk day the English plan is adopted, the buyers eagerly bidding against each other. In each case the principle is the same, the avoidance of the initiative being aimed at. And every business man knows that the same principle runs through all transactions. No man says, " I will give you £1,000 for your house," but, " What do you want for your house?" and the seller replies, "What will you give me?" each trying to avoid taking the initiative in naming a price.

Mr. Mill's argument should, therefore, run thus, that the employers suffering under the necessity of taking the initiative are at a great disadvantage, and require some artificial arrangements to give them even a chance of contending successfully against the labourers. His premises being the exact reverse of the fact, the conclusion we arrive at is the opposite of his. The labourers are under no disadvantage from not having the initiative, but the reverse.

But although Mr. Mill lays great stress on this supposed disadvantage, which I have proved to be on the other side, I do not attach much weight to it either way. The fact is, that in a sensitive market the initiative or want of it is of very little importance, and men do not spend much time in trying to avoid it. I say in a sensitive market. Now, what is a market? At page 38 of Professor Marshall's *Principles of Economics*, a market is defined to be "the whole of any region in which buyers and sellers are in such free intercourse with one another that the prices of the same goods tend to equality easily and quickly." And the essential point to make a sensitive market is that there should be a large number of transactions in the same goods.

Now, although I think I have disproved all that Mr. Mill asserts up to this point, let us suppose that we were to admit for the sake of argument all that he contends for. That is, let us admit that the law of supply and demand does not work with exactness, and that the inexactness tells against the labourers. The next question is, will the remedy which Mr. Mill proposes, the combination of labourers, mitigate the evil? On the contrary, it will and does enormously aggravate it.

Admitting the inexactness, it is at its maximum in articles where there are few transactions, such as estates, houses, pictures, horses, &c., and at its minimum where there is a keen and sensitive market. The best examples of the latter are perhaps the cotton market and the market for consols. Both these articles are quoted in variations of a fraction of 1 per cent., about $\frac{1}{4}$ to $\frac{1}{2}$ per cent., and no man would think of saying that he had got the best or worst of the bargain, as long as he got the market price. One-eighth per cent. on £1,000, the price of the house Mr. Llewellyn Smith spoke of, would be 25s., not an amount worth using much *finesse* or force to gain. And the sensitiveness of the market depends upon the number of individual transactions. In a well-known stock in which there is much dealing a London jobber will either buy or sell with a margin of $\frac{1}{8}$ per cent. either way. In a less known stock where there are few transactions he might want 3 or 4 per cent. of a margin.

The more numerous the transactions are the smaller are the variations in price between one transaction and another, and the want of exactness of which Mr Mill complains is reduced to an infinitesimal quantity. But Mr. Mill's remedy—combination among labourers—destroys the labour market altogether, as it does away with the number of individual transactions, and substitutes a system of few transactions between a master and all his workmen at a time, or between all the masters on one hand and all the men on the other. It thus removes labour from the category of things in the price of which there is a minimum of inexactness and puts it among those where the small number of transactions causes a maximum of uncertainty. I should not put the labour market in the category of the most sensitive. In no case would the rate of wages fluctuate like the price of stocks or produce. The action of the law, though delicate, is not rapid. But at all events combination by reducing the number of transactions does enormously increase the no-man's-land, the area of uncertainty in the labour market. Mr. Mill's remedy thus greatly aggravates the evil which he wishes to cure, or rather I should say combination creates an evil where none existed before. It is often said that the work of trades' unions is just the higgling of the market. But as we have seen, a market involves a number of buyers and sellers, and a number of transactions. Combination destroys this market, and in doing so it destroys a gauge of the true price, delicate, sensitive, and self-acting, and, as Mr. Mill and Professor Marshall admit, almost perfect; and it puts nothing in its place. By the law of supply and demand the proper wage in any trade would be the wage at which a sufficient number of labourers, acting individually, could be found to do the work properly. That I think is a perfect rule. Mr. Mill and Mr. Llewellyn Smith think it not far from perfect, for you will observe that none of the economical authorities share the extreme views of those who believe trades' unions, new or old, are going to do great things for the working classes. Professor Marshall in his address at Leeds the other day said that while combination could do something in raising wages it could not do much. But for this rule, which, while admitting it to be almost perfect, they discard, what do they substitute? They have nothing to put in its place. Trades' unions have no principle by which to fix the proper remuneration for labour. It should just be something more than it is. If the wage is 5d. an hour, it should be 6d.; if it is 8d. it should be 10d. To ask an advance when they think trade is good, and if necessary to enforce it by a strike is their only principle. Professor Marshall, indeed, in his book, and Mr. Mavor, in his paper on wages' theories, speak of the need of collecting statistics, with the view of ascertaining what is the proper share of labour in distribution. But I believe that would be an impossible task. Any one who reads Professor Marshall's Book (Book VII., Caps. 4, 5, 6) will see how difficult it would be to say what the rate of wages should be in any trade or place. Nothing short of omniscience, perfect honesty, perfect impartiality, and perfect judgment would be sufficient for the task.

It may be objected to the foregoing argument that the increasingly imperfect mobilisation of labour and capital — due on the one hand to the specialisation of labour, and on the other to the increased expense of machinery—would tend to counteract the diminution of the market range, which would be effected by the giving up of combination. But two blacks do not make a white; and even if it were true that the immobility complained of made the market less sensitive, that would not be a reason for adopting or retaining an arrangement which makes it less sensitive still. And, while I admit the increasing immobility in regard to capital, I do not think it is the case that labour is less mobile than before. For, though specialisation tends in that direction, cheapness of travelling, quicker and better information, better education, and, consequently, greater adaptability tend all the other way. (See Marshall, p. 602).

On this point, General Walker, the great American economist, says — "Remembering that the one thing to be secured for the proper distribution of wealth is *perfect competition*, in judging of any act or measure, it should be enquired whether it will on the whole and in the long run increase or diminish the substantial, not the nominal, freedom of movement." With that principle I thoroughly agree, but I cannot go with General Walker when he seems to think that, in order that the law of supply and demand should work properly, it would be necessary that labour should be perfectly mobile, that every labourer should be perfectly informed, perfectly alive to his interests, and perfectly willing and able to go to the locality where he could sell his labour to the best advantage. I hold that something far short of that is all that is necessary. If there are a few in each trade or each congested locality willing to change or to send out their sons to other places or trades, that is all that is needed to redress the balance.

No one can say that, in Scotland at least, we have not these necessary conditions.

In a Scotch labourer's or workman's family there are often, I might almost say generally, as many occupations as there are members of the family.

But even if labour were so immobile as to be divided into a number of separate little groups, the law of supply and demand would still be applicable to each of these groups within itself. And if it is complained that labour is less mobile than capital (which I do not think is the case) there is all the more reason for labourers doing everything to attract, and avoiding anything (as trade unions) likely to drive away capital, seeing that it is thought labour cannot follow.

I agree with General Walker that the great desideratum is perfect competition, and while that is not attainable our aim should be to make it as nearly perfect as we can. But trades' unionism, which he seems to approve of as a remedy, does the very reverse. Its aim is to restrict competition, and in this it is only too successful. I knew a plumber who went to London lately for his wife's health. He was told he would not be allowed to work till he joined the union. He offered to join, and was told he could not do so till he had worked three months in a union shop. He asked what he was to do, and was told to go home to Scotland, and had to do so. That is a typical case of trades' unionism action, and is surely not in the direction of perfect competition, nor of either nominal or substantial freedom of movement.

It will now be convenient to leave Mr. Mill for a little, and to consider some of the other arguments for combination, returning to Mr. Mill's paper later on. The answer to Mr. Fawcett's complaint that wages do not rise immediately with an improvement in trade is very simple. A rise or fall in wages ought not to, and does not naturally, coincide in point of time with an improvement or depression in trade. Trade is brisk and profits good for some time before employers extend their operations, build more ships, mills, &c.; and it is only then that more men are wanted, and wages rise naturally, and would do so without the help of a union; and a premature demand for an advance has the effect of checking these extended operations, and so limiting the ultimate demand for labour.

On the other hand, trade is bad, and masters are making little profit, and often suffering loss for some time before they curtail their work; and it is only then (or when the natural increase of labourers overtakes the demand) that men are found to be super-abundant, and wages fall. If the men are at an apparent disadvantage when trade improves, they have at least as great a corresponding advantage when it falls off.

But again, as Professor Marshall says, every employer of labour is himself equal to a combination of workmen, and the tendency of to-day is towards amalgamation of large concerns, concentration of trades into few hands. To meet these great combinations the men, it is said, must combine, or they would be crushed.

The necessity is purely imaginary. We must remember that the labour in any trade is not a fixed quantity. It is constantly varying. Men are dying, leaving the country, leaving the town, giving up work for a great variety of reasons, and others taking their places. Besides that, there are a number of men—a kind of fringe, as it were, on the borders of every trade—who will be tempted to work when the wages are good, and fall away when the wages are bad.

Now, suppose, to take an extreme case, that all the masters in a trade were to amalgamate, so that there should be only one employer against many thousands of workmen, and therefore no rival establishments competing for the men's labour. Suppose that the one employer was paying 30s. a week, and he gradually finds (for in a normal state of things these changes in the labour market are very gradual, though, under combination, very violent) his foreman telling him men are getting scarce—that some are leaving, and no new men taking their places. He is obliged to raise the wage to 31s.—and if that is not sufficient, to 32s., to bring up the inducements to enter his service to the level of the competing employments around him. On the other hand, when trade generally is slack, the foreman will report a superabundance of men applying at the gates, and few vacancies occurring; and now is the time for a reduction of wages. Even then there is no need for the men to strike. They may rest assured that if the reduction is not justified by the facts, the facts will soon assert themselves. The supply of men will fall off, and the rate will have to be raised again.

But it is said combination enables the men to put a reserve price on their labour which they could not otherwise do. Well, I have said that the true economical wage is the wage necessary to attract a sufficient number of men able to do the work properly; or, in other words, it is the real reserve price put upon

2

their labour by the men in the trade who are in the strongest position for bargaining—or, in case I may be thought to be begging the question, it is admittedly very near that reserve price.

Let us see how that works. Suppose that there are 3,000 men of a certain degree of skill wanted in a trade, and that 2,000 would be forthcoming at a wage of 25s., 2200 at 26s., and 200 more coming forward for each additional shilling offered, until, to secure the last 200, the wage of 30s. has to be paid. Well, the wage in that trade will be 30s. Thus the wages are fixed by the real reserve price of the last batch of men required. These men are the strongest men in the trade, economically. They may have money saved, or they may have no families, or they may think of emigrating, or may have some other employment to which they can readily turn. From whatever cause, they are in a strong position for bargaining, and they practically do the bargaining for the whole trade. Any attempt to crush the weaker men by reducing the wages would drive these strong men away, and the wages would have to be raised to retain them.

Now, does combination give the men a stronger weapon than that? I think not. Combination does not enable the men to put a real reserve price on their labour, but only a fictitious or temporary price fixed arbitrarily, for the purpose of bargaining. Probably not a tenth of the labourers would, if it came to the push, really make that the reserve price. The employer knows that, and is thereby challenged to a trial of endurance, with the certainty that, if he declines the challenge and submits, he will shortly have a further demand made upon him. Therefore he must show fight. Now, this method provides no test of the real reserve price which any portion of the labourers put on their services; and even if it did so, it would surely be a most expensive method, when, by simply doing nothing, the real reserve price of the most independent men in the trade would shortly manifest itself. And notice that these strong men of whom I speak, if they cast in their lot with the other men in a strike, exhaust their resources, and are no longer in such a strong position for bargaining. And further, it is a very dangerous thing to put forward a fictitious reserve price, as there is a risk of thereby losing the market altogether. Now, a real reserve price implies that you do not greatly regret the loss of the employment; but it might be a very serious matter if the men in a strike were taken at their word, and the work given up—and that is the cause of all the bitter feeling in strikes.

Professor Nicholson, in his essay on wages, says—"At the time of the Tudors the decay of many towns was largely due to these 'fraternities of evil,' as Bacon called the guilds. The history of the craft guilds is full of instructive examples of the principles governing wages. No doubt their regulations tended to raise wages above their natural rate ; but, as a natural consequence, industries migrated to places where the oppressive regulations did not exist." In other words, their combination enabled them to fix a reserve price, but it was a false one, and therefore dangerous. The craft guild is the prototype of the trades' union. The latter helped to drive shipbuilding from the Thames, and the lace curtain trade from Nottingham, and now threatens to ruin the port of London.

But it may be said, what is sauce for the goose is sauce for the gander. If it does the men no harm for masters to combine, why should you object to men combining? Why should not all the men in a trade combine, and fix the terms for the masters? Well, there would be no objection to that, if it were possible. The essential point is to preserve a market by the multiplicity of transactions. If employers were all what used to be called "wee corks," employing two or three men, if they were sufficiently small units to make the dealings with them very numerous, I believe the law would work perfectly with all the men combined and the masters uncombined, and the masters would not suffer at all from their isolation.* But that is not possible. Each master is too large a unit for the dealings with the employers to be numerous enough

* In that case the combined men would be the employers and the masters the employed. But management would be divorced from risk, which would be a fatal arrangement.

to make a market. The market can only be preserved, therefore, by the men remaining uncombined, and, as I have shown, they would not suffer thereby in the slightest degree. And notice here that while masters must make the general conditions of their employment such as to attract men to fill the vacancies as they occur, which is a perfect check upon masters' tyranny and low wages, there is no corresponding check upon the tyranny of trades' unions. Once they have the upper hand they may, and often do, go on without any check, till they have ruined the industry and themselves with it.

And here I may remark that it seems to be generally assumed that employers have a great advantage in bargaining over workmen, because of their greater power of holding out. Economists write as if a total or partial stoppage of work meant to an employer only a little less profit at the end of a year, while to the workmen it is a question of life and death for himself and his family. Now, men of business know that most employers work largely with borrowed capital, and that their own capital is often only a small part of the total amount employed. They must pay interest on their borrowed capital, and a stoppage of work through a strike, or a number of machines standing idle for want of workers, often means not less profit, but an absolute loss, and if long continued, total ruin. If not the employer's life, his business life is at stake, and there is not in human experience a keener anguish to a sensitive and honourable man than the fear of impending bankruptcy; grief for the loss of nearest and dearest friends, or the fear of death itself is not more poignant. I consider that the labourer, who can generally move from one employment to another, is at no disadvantage in bargaining with the employer, who is tied to his machines, which he must keep fully employed or perish financially. But all this about the power of holding out is bad economy. A labourer should not go idle an hour longer than is necessary for looking out for other employment, nor should an employer adopt the policy of holding out by keeping his machinery standing. And neither of them would think of doing so, but for this combination theory.

We now come to the power of resisting tyranny in other matters than mere wages, which combination is said to give.

If business is to be carried on at all, the responsible managers must have the power of dismissal, or there is an end of all discipline, and we reach a state of chaos such as is at present to be seen in the London docks. Mr. Mill says to extract real work from day labourers without the power of dismissal is not practicable. And as the greater includes the less, the right of dismissal includes the right of every legal act up to that point. If anything illegal is done, there are the courts of law to appeal to, or the labourer has the right of withdrawal. It may be said that a poor labourer cannot go to law, and that is often true. In the absence of Mr. Herbert Spencer's plan of free law, a union of workers for paying expenses of lawsuits would be a legitimate arrangement. But the appeal should be to the law. An appeal to a trades' union executive, an *imperium in imperio*, is not satisfactory, and is dangerous to the state. Such a tribunal throws discredit on the law, usurps its functions, and is certain to be both incompetent and unjust. Without attributing to him a double dose of original sin, a trades' union secretary has more power than should be in the hands of any man, even a Lord Chief Justice.

For minor annoyances not reaching to legal wrong, the best remedy is to do nothing. I will illustrate this from our business experience.

I daresay we have all come across large wealthy houses who are most overbearing and tyrannical in their dealings with smaller firms. We have all known merchants who treat travellers with the greatest rudeness, who pay little attention to their appointments, who make unfair deductions from their accounts, reject goods without due cause, decline to pay accounts when due, and will listen to no expostulation on these points, but simply refer the complainer to his legal remedy. Is it ever thought necessary for the small firms to combine against those men? Certainly not! Their unreasonable conduct soon comes to be discounted, and they have to pay for it in some form or another. They never get the first offer of bargains, they have to pay more for their regular purchases, or they are left to unscrupulous dealers, who take the profit out of them by cheating, which is not to be got by fair dealing. I have heard a very shrewd and keen salesman say of such a man—" Well, that is the very kind of man I want to do with. If no one else can get on with him, I will make it my business to do so, and I will make much more out of him than I can out of a decent fellow for whose account Tom, Dick, and Harry are all competing." It is the same with the tyrannical employer. He soon gets to be known. There is no need for combination against him. He cannot get the best men unless he pays more for them. He has to pay more or put up with the poor workmen, the drinkers, and bad characters.

Justice is far more likely to be meted out to men and masters alike by this method than under any system of trades' union supervision. In some unions no choice is allowed. The first man on the books must be taken, and thus good men get bad masters and good masters bad men.

In regard to Professor Nicholson's idea that, while trades' unions can do little towards raising nominal wages, they can raise the real rate of wages, he gives no reasons for that opinion, and I think it is quite unwarranted. It seems to me that so far as any improvement in the condition of workmen trenches upon profits, it is subject to the law of supply and demand even more certainly than a rise in nominal wages.

But it may be said, " by their fruits ye shall know them." The trades' unions have raised wages. Well, a gradual rise in wages has taken place along with the existence of trades' unions; but it does not follow that the one is a consequence of the other. *Post hoc sed non propter hoc.* We see some occupations, the workers in which have no union, and yet have got almost as great a rise as those in the united trades. Some unionists say that the rise which they have secured has sent up the wages in all trades. But their own economist, Mr. Mill, says that a rise gained by restriction of numbers is at the expense of non-union workers. If, therefore, we find these non-unionists getting a substantial rise, the inference is that they would have got a still greater one if there had been no unions, and that, therefore, there has been a natural rise of wages all round independently of the unions. Steam, railways, telegraphs, have enabled the accumulation of capital to outrun population during the past generation, and the competition of enriched capitalists for labourers' services has raised wages.

As to a limitation of the hours of labour by trades' union rules, I think such limitation in the case of adult male labour most undesirable; but if it is to be undertaken at all, ~~I agree~~ with Sir-Charles ~~Dilke that it should~~ be done by ~~the State. It should be the expression in law~~ of the opinion ~~of the whole~~ community, for sanitary and social reasons, and should not be attempted by each trade, under a short-sighted and mistaken idea that wages will thereby be raised or more men employed.*

I will now return to Mr. Mill's argument on the wages fund theory, but before doing so I will notice a remark made by Mr. Llewellyn Smith which was not in his paper, but was received with great approval by some members of this section. He said that wages are not paid out of capital at all. General Walker and some other modern economists hold that view, but I think they have quite failed to prove their case, and there is at present a decided reaction against them. The doctrine is well, and, I think, conclusively controverted by Mr. Macvane in the American *Quarterly Journal of Economics*, which is to be found in the library of this Society.

Professor Nicholson says that wages may be said to be paid partly out of capital and partly out of produce. And Professor Marshall says the dispute about the wages fund theory is very much a question of words.

If wages are not paid out of capital, but out of produce, where do they come from when there is no produce? Suppose a capitalist

---

* "If reduction of hours results in decreased production wages will fall, other things being equal. If reduction of hours results in maintenance of production per man there will be no additional employment, other things being equal."—*Mavor.*

should sink a mine for coal or gold, and the whole produce should be the knowledge that there is no coal or gold there, can the men's wages be paid out of that knowledge? In the whaling industry the men are fed and paid monthly wages, and in addition so much per ton of oil, whalebone, and sealskins. If the ship should return clean, that part of the men's pay depending on the produce is saved, but the monthly wages and keep are paid from capital and never repaid to it. And where there is produce what do the labourers live upon during the weeks or months or even years which pass in some businesses before there is any return? If a man should sit down to write a book on political economy which will take him two or three years, and has no appointments, what does he live on in the meantime? He must live on his capital. If he has no capital he cannot undertake the work, unless some other man advances him capital, or hires him to do the work, in which case the second party pays his wages out of capital. It may be for a week or it may be for a year, but every employer makes arrangements to lay aside part of his capital to pay wages till his returns come in. But whether wages are paid out of capital or not, the extent of the manufacturing or industrial operations which any employer can engage in is determined by the amount of the capital which he has or can command, and is willing to employ in that way.

The correctness of the wages fund theory is not at all necessary for my position. If the rate of wages is determined even approximately by supply and demand that is quite sufficient for the argument. And no economical authority denies that they are so determined within a certain range.

Mr. Mill's objection to the wages fund theory is not of this absolute kind. He says that there is no definite part of capital which can be properly so called, but that all an employer's floating capital, even that which he designed for himself and his family, is available for the payment of wages if necessary, and he goes on to say the limit of the amount the employer may be forced to pay in wages is not the inexorable limits of the wages fund, but how much would ruin him or force him to abandon the business.

Mr. Mill here again takes a very short view. For, while it is true that a capitalist employer may be forced to pay an amount in wages which will leave him only a bare subsistence, it is certain that other capitalists will not engage in business with such a prospect before them. No man would deny himself to save, and then endure the anxieties of business, if he is only thereby to get a bare subsistence, which he can get as a labourer. Men will save money and go into business just in proportion to the inducement to do so, to the prospect of the profit to be gained. Therefore, although isolated employers may have to pay more than they intended as their wages fund, that fund cannot be indefinitely increased from profits.

Mr. Mill's correction of the wages fund theory, while true of individual cases, is again, on the whole, quite the reverse of the truth, and his argument based on it quite unsound. The theory he previously taught was the true one. An increase in wages reduces profits, and reduces the inducement to save and extend business, and this again tends to a reduction of wages.

Professor Marshall says, page 298—"A fall in the rate of interest does, in general, tend to check the accumulation of wealth;" at page 299 he says—"A rise in the rate of interest increases the desire to save;" and at page 616—"The rate of interest *cannot fall* below that limit at which it offers only just sufficient inducement to those who are on the margin of doubt whether they will save or not." The amount of saving will depend upon the inducement given—*i.e.*, on the rate of profits interest.

Thus, in direct contradiction to Mr. Mill, there is a law of nature making it inherently impossible for wages to rise to the point of absorbing the fund which the employers, *on the whole*, intend to devote to the carrying on of their business, and also of what they allow for their private expenses as well, beyond the mere necessaries of life. Ricardo says the employer's motive for accumulation will diminish with every diminution of profit, and will cease altogether when their profits are so low as not to afford them an adequate compensation for their trouble and risk. And as the increase or, in the face of an increasing population, the keeping up of wages depends upon a proportionate increase of capital and employment of it in business, it follows that, if wages were so high as to absorb all but a bare subsistence to the capitalist, they must rapidly fall with every addition to the population.

Well, let us see how far we have got.

Mr. Mill's theory of the inexactness of the operation of the law of supply and demand is wrong.

His theory of the advantage of the initiative is the reverse of the truth.

His remedy for the supposed inexactness—combination—increases it.

A rise in wages should not necessarily coincide with an improvement in trade.

Combination does not increase the men's power of bargaining, nor is it a proper or effective shield from tyranny.

It cannot be proved that trades' unions have raised wages.

If men's working hours are to be restricted it should be by the State.

Mr. Mill's objection to the wages fund theory is without foundation.

I have up to this time been speaking of open unions. I do not deny that, by restricting their numbers, some trades have managed to secure high wages; and we will now consider Mr. Mill's justification of the restriction of the number of labourers in a trade, as practised by trades' unions. He admits that all that he has maintained will be of no avail in keeping up wages unless the number of competitors for employment can be limited. The rise in wages, he says, must be at the expense either of wages in other departments or of profits, and in general both will contribute. I have shown, I think, that profits cannot be made to bear a share of it without re-acting upon wages, so that in reality the rise of wages in one department will be solely at the expense of wages in other departments. Even Mr. Mill admits that it will be partly so; and he justifies that by the plea that unions of particular trades are necessary steps towards a universal union including all labour. And this is an argument which has been adopted by many economists. But I think it will not stand a moment's examination. What is aimed at is a limitation of the amount of labour in each trade. It is evident that, for such limitation, a union of all labour is exactly the same as no union at all, while a union not of all labour, but of all trades, will create an enormous army of paupers. Let us suppose that the union officials should consider the excess of labour in an open trade to be 10 per cent. of the whole, which is a moderate estimate, from their point of view. The surplus men from one trade could not be absorbed by other trades, for these are also organised and occupied in getting rid of their own surplus.

Suppose there are thirty trades in the country with an average of 200,000 men in each—6,000,000 in all—and 2,000,000 unskilled labourers. A restriction of numbers by 10 per cent. in all these trades would add 600,000 men to the ranks of unskilled labourers. But unskilled labour is also, we are told, to be organised and limited in the future, and a beginning has been made in that direction with the dock labourers. Unskilled labour, then, will refuse the surplus 600,000 men from other trades, and will add its own surplus 200,000 to the ranks of the unemployed, making in all 800,000. Those 800,000 men with their families—say 3,000,000 of people—would be paupers to be kept at the public expense, of which, of course, the employed men would have to bear their share. Restrictive union is then a weapon directed against a part of the labouring class,·and cannot be reconciled with their interests either present or future.

So much for Mr. Mill's first apology for what he calls "an oligarchy of manual labourers indirectly supported by a tax levied on the democracy."

His second plea is, as I quoted, that the blacklegs or knobsticks, the men who are excluded, are a morally inferior class, putting no restraint on their additions to the population. "We do them no wrong," he makes his labour oligarchs say, "by intrenching ourselves behind a barrier to exclude those whose competition would bring down our wages without more than momentarily raising theirs, but only adding to the total number in existence." Mr. Mill calls this the Malthusian theory, which I think is a libel on Mr. Malthus. Mr. Malthus advocated self-restraint. He never proposed the destruction of the weak by the strong, in order that the latter should have more to divide.

We have heard of strong men on board a castaway ship seizing all the food and leaving the weaker members of the crew to starve, but I never before heard such conduct approved of because they were morally superior.

The right to labour in any system of morality that I know of is indefeasible, and the right to give employment equally so, but the unionist says to men, "you shall not work," and to masters, "you shall not be allowed to give work." Slavery itself was more humane. And who is to be the judge of the moral superiority of the unionist. The unionists themselves apparently. I do not deny that there are many able and even disinterested men in their ranks, but are the mass of them so much superior to non-unionists even in the matter of reckless adding to the population as to entitle them to take this high ground. Is the riveter more moral than the light porter or the clerk? Does he drink less, smoke less, has he fewer children? If he were inclined to save he might easily become a capitalist himself without robbing the poor blackleg. According to Mr. Mill, the intelligent artisan has no duties to his employer, nor any to his non-unionist neighbour; all his moral obligations are towards himself and his fellow-unionists. I surely need say no more to prove that restrictive unionism is quite indefensible from a moral point of view.

We have now seen on what insufficient grounds the belief that trades' unions can raise general wages rests. Let us next ask what is the cost to the community and workmen in particular? In the first place, there is the disturbance to trade, not only from stoppage of supplies, but also from violent fluctuations in prices. When miners' wages are jumping up and down 40 per cent. to 50 per cent. in a few months, and the coal supply restricted, and prices varying in the same way, every industry is injuriously affected.*

Then there is the weekly or monthly contribution to the society funds. And next there is the loss of wages during strikes, which often swallows up all the apparent gain. But more important even than these is the diminished demand for labour. Every strike, or threat of a strike; every letter from a trades' union secretary; everything that makes the position of an employer less profitable, less agreeable, less honourable, has its effect in checking the demand for labour. Loss by strikes must now be an element in the calculations of every intending employer, and may, and often does, turn the scale in deciding him not to go into business. The competition of capitalists for labour, and not combination, is the labourers true strength. Their policy should be to make the position of employers as pleasant and profitable as possible, and to

---

* In New Zealand and Australia, where they carry things to their logical conclusions more quickly than we do here, the boycott ordered by the trades' unions at the present time is in as full force and as far reaching as it is in Tipperary. One case in New Zealand is worth notice.

Messrs. Whitcombe & Tombs, Christchurch, having had a dispute with the Typographical Society, were boycotted. The Port of Lyttleton was ordered not to have any dealings with the offending firm, and the officials not complying the Port was boycotted. Next, the Union Steamship Co. was boycotted for sailing to Lyttleton, and all its men withdrawn; then the railway followed, and then the miners were withdrawn from the pits which supplied the steamers, and even the pumping operations threatened with suspension, to the permanent ruin of the works, and all merchants and shopkeepers dealing with any of the boycotted concerns were boycotted also. Mr Miller, the Secretary of the Maritime Council, said that "the first man made to suffer by dismissal or suspension will be the signal for everything to stop from Auckland to the Bluff." Thus, in the good time coming, which trades' unionists promise us, every petty quarrel between a tradesman and his men, or even with one man, is to be a universal quarrel between all capital and all labour, and unless the former submit at once, the whole work of the country is to cease. Surely this is the *reductio ad absurdum* of trades' unionism; but yet it is the logical and inevitable outcome of the principle of combination. Champion, Burns, and Hyndman see this, and are apparently deliberately carrying it to its absurd conclusion, so that it may discredit the principle of freedom of action, and may cause people to turn to socialism for relief.

coax them into trade, just as a shopkeeper tries to entice customers into his shop. Once in trade, nothing could prevent them competing with each other for the labourers services. Instead of that the policy they adopt is to harass the employers as much as possible, "*pour encourager les autres.*" A parallel to their behaviour would be that of a shopkeeper who should keep a dog to worry those customers who decline to pay his prices. He might congratulate himself on his success with those who are in his shop, as the men often do at the end of a strike; but he would not thereby extend or maintain his connection, nor do they. I have no doubt that many hundreds of millions of money, which might have been profitably employed at home, have been driven abroad by the fear of trades' unions. Profits have to be increased, and are increased, to pay for all these risks and annoyances, and wages are trenched upon to that extent. In addition to that, employers are less able to give employment, their capital having been partly lost.

Then the grinding tyranny of the unions over the men is another feature of combination. Mr. Fred. Harrison, in a magazine article, glorying in the success of the dock strike, said it would have collapsed in a fortnight "but for the pickets." That proves that he believes that a large number, perhaps a minority, perhaps even a large majority, of the men wished to work but dared not. Every man was watched by the pickets, and knew that, if he dared to act for himself, he would be a marked man, and life would be made a burden to him. Mr. Llewellyn Smith denied this, and said that pickets were necessary to meet strangers at railway stations and explain matters to them. Well, I should think 500 men would be ample for that work. But there were 11,000 on picket duty daily. What were the odd 10,500 doing? The boasted order of the great dock strike was like that of the conqueror who made a wilderness and called it peace.

Again, combination fosters class prejudice and hatred. It makes the bargaining no longer a contest between capital and labour, two impersonal forces, which, if left to themselves, will find their own level, but often a fiercely passionate personal struggle between capitalists and labourers. Professor Marshall says (p. 409)— "Anger and vanity, jealousy and offended pride, are at least as common causes of strikes and lockouts as the desire for procuring gain." And this is the unionists' ideal method of making a bargain! In such a contest, when prudence is thrown to the winds, the longest purse is sure to have the best of it.

I sat one night last winter at a public meeting next a respectable working man, who, each time that a reference was made to landlords and capitalists, kept saying to himself in a solemn tone of deep conviction, "Hell will be their portion." Mr. Gray, the manager of Silvertown rubber works, who is known to many of us in Glasgow as a singularly large-minded and warm-hearted man, was, during the strike of the Company's workers last year, each day held up to public odium in the columns of the London newspapers as a low, mean, sneaking ruffian, a murderer of women and children, and the men were quoted as hoping that they would be stokers in hell that they might give it to him hot.

Mr. Llewellyn Smith made light of this, and said the men's language was strong in proportion to the poverty of their vocabulary. They seemed to me to have a very copious vocabulary. But I do not think Mr. Smith or any of us would like to pass through such an ordeal, and I ask you if these feelings are the natural ones between buyer and seller, or such as would exist between master and man, without combination. Under combination the most benevolent employer is liable to have such an experience any day.

It has also been said that this view too exclusively regards labour as a commodity of the same nature as other commodities. Well, no doubt there is a distinction in the fact that the seller, the labourer, cannot be separated from his labour, from the commodity which he sells. But that seems to me to be a distinction without a difference. I have never learned how that distinction makes it more necessary for the sellers of labour to combine than other sellers, or makes their commodity less subject to the law of supply and demand. Labour resembles in some respects perishable commodities, and the holding of it back from the market in strikes is very bad economy.

Well, I have tried to show that by open combination the men cannot get any advantage, and that when some of them do so by restrictive means it is at the expense of the rest of the working class. Even if they got all that the economists who favour combination allege—*i.e.*, a chance of obtaining a slightly larger share of a very narrow margin of price—I ask would the game be worth the candle, at the cost of great disturbance of trade, driving away of capital, cost of organisation, loss of wages in strikes, tyranny over men, and class jealousy and hatred. I think not.

Now, I would ask, not the economists, but those who believe in labour receiving a much larger share of the produce of industry, where is it to come from? Professor Marshall estimates the average rate of interest at present at 3 per cent., and that would seem to be high enough, as the Chancellor of the Exchequer can get as much money as he likes at $2\frac{3}{4}$ per cent. Well, if the increase of capital just keeps pace with the increase of population at that rate, by how much can the demands of labour decrease that rate without the increase of capital being checked and falling below the needs of an increasing population. You may say our great manufacturers earn much more than 3 per cent. So many of them do, but if you allow for wages of management and *for risk of loss and of failure*, it is probable that they do not earn much more on the average. For every one of the great successful firms which bulk largely in the public eye, there are thousands which have gone to the wall. There is not a well-to-do man among us who has not many relatives and friends who have lost all they had in business. There is a large joint stock Coal Company, the 20 per cent. dividend of which was often quoted last year as a reason for a rise in miners' wages. But that Company paid a dividend then for the first time in the fourteen years of its existence and had written off as loss £100,000 of its capital, and after all the 20 per cent. was only on the reduced capital of £3 instead of £10. And the average earning of the Company was, therefore, instead of 20 per cent., less than one-half per cent. per annum.

Professor Marshall says (page 658)—"The number of those who succeed in business is but a small percentage of the whole ; and in their hands are concentrated the fortunes of others several times as numerous as themselves, who have made savings of their own or who have inherited the savings of others and lost them all, together with the fruits of their own efforts in unsuccessful business.

" In order, therefore, to find the average profits of a trade, we must not divide the aggregate profits by the number of those who are reaping them, nor even by that number added to the number who have failed, but from the aggregate profits of the successful, we must subtract the aggregate losses of those who have failed, and perhaps disappeared from the trade ; and we must then divide the remainder by the sum of the numbers of those who have succeeded and those who have failed. It is probable that the true gross earnings of management—that is, the excess of profits over interest —is not on the average more than a half, and in some risky trades not more than a tenth part of what it appears to be to persons who form their estimate of the profitableness of a trade by observation only of those who have secured its prizes."

Now, when we remember that in all these unsuccessful ventures the men are getting their steady wages all the time at a rate which leaves for profits, with minimum risk, not much more than 3 per cent.,* it seems to me that there is not much room for a great advance out of profits, and also that the men are much better off with a fixed weekly wage than they could be under any system of profit and loss sharing.

Of course all that I have said about men's trades' unions applies also to trades' unions for women, with this in addition—

It is in the highest degree desirable that women should be able

* It is difficult to estimate the earnings of management, or profits beyond interest. In some businesses it is very large, but on the average, counting failures, very small. The experience of many men, who have invested in shares of joint-stock companies, is that they would have been richer if they had never done so but lent their money at a low rate of interest ; and if you attack the profits of the more successful firms you reduce the average, and the rate of interest also.

to work for themselves, and not have to look to marriage as their sole way of escape from dependence. Therefore, the extension of the sphere of women's labour which has taken place of late years is most gratifying. This movement has been greatly helped, though not intentionally,* by the men's unions. Masters have turned, in weariness at the demands of the men, to female labour. There is only one thing that is likely to check or retard the still further development of women's industry, and that is the institution of women's trades' unions. That they are unnecessary is shown by the fact that no class in the community has secured a greater improvement in its condition than that of domestic servants, and that without any concerted action. The source from which improvement has been coming, and from which alone it can come—namely, the greater demand for female labour—will be weakened by the union. Masters will not see the advantage of exchanging the yoke of a male for that of a female union secretary. And if the women's league gets the domestic servants to combine, that will cause many people to give up housekeeping, and adopt the American plan of living in hotels and boarding-houses, and so reduce the demand for female servants.

I should have liked to discuss the principle of the sliding scale, and also of Boards of Conciliation and Arbitration, but have not left myself time. I will, however, say a few words. And first in regard to the sliding scale, by which the price, say of coal, and miners' wages are tied together. This, in my opinion, is a most clumsy and unscientific contrivance, and sure to break down. There is no natural immediate connection between the price of coal and miners' wages. Suppose a large new convenient coalfield were to be discovered and worked. That would increase the supply of coal and lower the price, while at the same time it would increase the demand for men and raise their wages. The price of coal and

---

* An employer in Glasgow was waited on not long ago by the officials of the union of his trade and told he had too many women in his shop and must dismiss some of them, and this although the work they were doing was work done admittedly everywhere by women.

the rate of wages cannot be tied together any more than the price of coal and the price of pit-props, and the same principle holds good in all other industries.

Then, as to arbitration, Professor Marshall says in his speech at Leeds — "The first point which Courts of Conciliation and Arbitration have to consider is, what are the rates of wages on the one hand, and profits on the other, which are required to call forth normal supplies of labour and capital; and only when that has been done can an enquiry properly be made as to the shares in which the two should divide between them the piece of good or ill fortune which has come to the trade."

Now, where, I ask, are the data for the first part of the inquiry to be found? A rough approximation might be got from the rate of labour in other occupations—that is, the market rate which at present partially rules price ; but, as combination goes on, and more and more destroys the market, even this rude method is closed. To suppose that such an inquiry could be conducted to any satisfactory issue is to beg the whole question. In my opinion it passes the wit of man. And why should the piece of good or ill fortune, instead of being roughly divided in this arbitrary fashion, not be left to take its natural course. It would fall first to capital, and then by an increased or diminished demand for labour, the latter would eventually, slowly but certainly, get or bear its share. In addition to this, arbitration and the sliding scale have this fatal fault, that they are both one-sided and unfair to the masters. If the price fixed is too high, the masters are bound to adhere to it; if too low, the men are not bound for a day. Even if their leaders observe the agreement, a number of the men will simply move away to other occupations, till the rate has to be raised to retain them.

What is the conclusion of the whole matter ? From my point of view, it is that, in fixing prices or wages, *laissez faire* is the true economical policy.

If that was true in the simpler times of the older economists, if it was then a mistake to attempt to fix prices arbitrarily, either by law or combination, much more is it the case now, when, to quote Mr. Mavor on the growing complexity of economical conditions, " though fundamental motives remain the same, they assume diversified forms, and enter into relations increasingly hard to disentangle."

Bargaining in wholesale by combination is a rough and barbarous process, combining a maximum of uncertainty with a maximum of loss by friction. A sensitive market—the result of a multiplicity of transactions—is the nearest possible approach to an ideal method of arriving at the true economic price of labour or anything else.

To quote our townsman, Mr. James Stirling of Cordale, who has written an admirable essay on this subject—" Free competition, by the unconscious moulding of human desires, brings about the same adjustment of industrial interests, as would be enjoined by morality on the conscious will."

30th January, 1891.

If the foregoing arguments are sound, no strike ever was or could be justifiable, no trades' union necessary or useful. Even the old unionism, moderately and carefully employed as it sometimes was by men like Mr. Broadhurst, has done much harm. But it cannot be kept within moderate bounds. It is gradually developing into what is called the new unionism. In this system the labourers in every trade are to join hands to help each other in coercing the capitalists in each trade separately. In every trade dispute the whole community is to be punished by a stoppage of all work till the decrees of the union leaders are obeyed in the smallest matters. In the railway strike which is now drawing to a close, an attempt was made to get all the other carrying trades to join in starving the community, so that they might force the railway managers to give way. The attempt failed, but in the moment of defeat the strike leaders tell us that they will be better organised and will win next time. And as I write, I read in this day's papers that a great strike of all the shipping and carrying trades in England is threatened involving the labour of a million men.

Apart from the fact that this new unionism will hurt the labourers by driving away capital, it surely needs no argument to prove that we are threatened with an intolerable tyranny.

The question arises, how can this be met? Evidently not by the law, as political power is now chiefly in the hands of the working classes, and they, generally speaking, approve of union methods. And even were it otherwise, it is probable that laws against combinations could not be re-enacted without an undue interference with liberty. Something, indeed, might be done, and, if there is any sense of fairness in our lawgivers, will be done to check the intimidation and outrage carried on under the name of picketing. But we must not expect much help from the law. The late examples of Australia and New Zealand, however, show us that the new unionism, if boldly met, can be successfully resisted. If the community * should realise its danger in time and make up its mind to discountenance and resist all combinations and strikes, to insist that the fixing of wages shall be left to the free competition of masters for men and men for employment, or even only to put down intimidation, all may yet be well. But if not, if the new unionism is allowed to get the upper hand, then it will not be our industry and commerce only that will be endangered, but our whole civilisation. Civilisations have before now suffered shipwreck, and, in my opinion, it is neither impossible nor improbable that trades-unionism may be the rock on which ours shall go to pieces.

* Other than the labourers.

420766

APPENDIX.

In reply to the criticisms of a correspondent on the first of his two Magazine articles, Mr. Mill wrote the following letter :—

AVIGNON, *May 17th*, 1869.

DEAR SIR,

I thank you for your letter, as I am always glad to have my opinions and arguments subjected to the criticism of any one who has studied the subject. It appears to me, however, that your remarks do not touch the scientific exactness of the propositions laid down in my article in the *Fortnightly Review*, but only the practical importance of the cases to which they are applicable. Now, though I am far from agreeing with you as to this, I have not discussed it in the article. My object, on this occasion, was to show that the door is not shut on the discussion of the subject by an insuperable law of nature.

It is one thing to say that labourers, by combination, *cannot* raise wages (which is the doctrine of many political economists), and another to say that it is not for their *interest* to force up wages so high as to reduce profits below what is a sufficient inducement to saving and to the increase of capital.

I have written a second article on the subject, which will be printed in the next number of the *Fortnightly*, and which, though it will not satisfy you on all points, will, I think, show you that I do not disregard either the moral or the prudential obligations of trades' unions.

I am, DEAR SIR,

Yours very faithfully,

J. S. MILL.

R. S. CREE, Esq.

In regard to the above it may be remarked that the only reason why it is not for the *interest* of the labourers to force up wages by combination is that, on the whole, and in the long run, they *cannot* thereby raise wages, but the reverse. It is not denied that they can sometimes do so temporarily, but they suffer for it in the long run.

Mr. Mill's distinction, therefore, is one without a real difference.

We have seen and discussed the observations promised here on the moral and prudential aspects of the question.